HERE COMES COWBOY LARRY, "STEPPING OUT IN FAITH"

By
Larry Callies with Michael D. Buford

HERE COMES COWBOY LARRY,
"STEPPING OUT IN FAITH"
By Larry Callies with Michael D. Buford

Published by:
Reality Marketing And Design
Toledo, OH 43606
www.realitymarketing.com

ISBN: 978-1-66783-881-6

Printed in the United States of America

I Dedicate this book
to all the young
Cowboys and Cowgirls
of all colors...

*Dream dreams
and then live them!*

*Larry Callies with his favorite horse, "Mister Smooth"

CONTENTS

FOREWORD

"Here Comes Cowboy Larry, STEPPING OUT IN FAITH," is a book written for children as an encouragement for them to continue to dream "their dreams" because they can become a reality. I am a Christian first, and a cowboy second! "Since it happened for me, I believe it could surely happen for them as well." This book is a testament that "dreams can still and will come true", especially when there is determination, faith, and action partnered with the dream. I was inspired by Michael D. Buford and Sarah Maslin Nir to share my story. Writing this book in my own words is another dream that has come true for me.

There is another reason why I wanted to write this book. My story gives a glimpse of the "hidden history" of the black cowboy of the Old West which is my heritage. As I share my life's story and the barriers I had to overcome to achieve my dream, some of the untold hardships of other black cowboys will also be revealed. It is my hope that the reader, if they have encountered hardships of any kind in achieving their dream, will come to the same conclusion that I did while pursuing mine. "A dream may be delayed, but it can never be destroyed. "

It is my pleasure to welcome you to go on a trail ride I have been traveling for nearly 68 years. My original dream of becoming a cowboy has come true. But once it became a reality, it opened the door for so many other dreams for which I am now living their realities today. Ride with me on your favorite horse and explore how the dream of "Cowboy Larry" came true. Along the way, you just might discover that your dream can become true too when partnered with determination, faith, and action.

"There are always two sides to a story —
one is the truth; one is a lie.
What side are you on?"
-Larry Callies

ACKNOWLEDGMENTS

I first want to acknowledge my parents, Mr. Leon and Mrs. Inell Callies, my grandpa, Mr. Nathan Callies, and my uncle, Mr. Willie Callies for the inspiration they have given me their entire lives to dream dreams. They told me that with the dream, I should always do the hard work and make the commitment to achieve the dream.

I want to also thank Preacher Williams and his son, Tex Williams, for the assistance they both have given me to develop the knowledge and skills to become a cowboy and for being the good role models as black cowboys to keep our heritage alive.

I would like to say special thanks to Mr. Sloan Williams, owner of one of the biggest ranches in Wharton County, Texas, for the opportunities he gave me as a young man to put into practice what I had learned about being a cowboy on his ranch and the rodeos I worked for him.

Finally, I would like to thank two special people who have come into my life since I opened THE BLACK COWBOY MUSEUM, Ms. Sarah Maslin Nir, writer for THE NEW YORK TIMES, and author of her own book, "Horse Crazy; and Reverend Michael D. Buford, publisher of THE GOOD NEWS MONTHLY, and also author of his book, "Up from Cotton." They both have inspired me to dream another dream of having my own book written and published about my life and the journey God took me on to see my dream of becoming a cowboy come true.

Larry Callies

Here Comes Cowboy Larry, "Stepping Out In Faith"

INTRODUCTION

HERE COMES COWBOY LARRY, "I HAVE ALWAYS WANTED TO BE A COWBOY!"

HERE COMES COWBOY LARRY, "STEPPING OUT IN FAITH," is the personal story of the life of Larry Callies becoming a cowboy growing up in Southeast Texas." His dream was met with many challenges beginning in elementary school with the unbelief and ridicule he received from his classmates and teachers about becoming a cowboy.

It was later discovered Larry had a learning disability during his elementary and high school years which affected him greatly in reading. While in college he discovered he had the learning disability known as, "dyslexia," which was another challenge he faced and dealt with on his journey to become a cowboy.

Larry also had to deal with the cultural beliefs and customs from both the black and white Texas communities during the 1950's and 1960's and the limitations they placed on him.

And finally, Larry had to face the existing laws of segregation that prohibited him from freely learning and participating in the craft he so much wanted to develop to become a cowboy.

Larry Callies, known as "Cowboy Larry" by family, friends, and strangers alike, dreamed at the age of 10 of becoming a cowboy like his dad, Leon Callies; and his famous kinfolks, "Preacher Williams" and future Hall of Famer, "Tex Williams."

Cowboy Larry has led an exciting life as a country western singer with his band, LARRY CALLIES AND THE BRONCO BAND; as a professional rodeo cowboy "calf roper and team roper," winning many awards; and being the founder of the famous, BLACK COWBOY MUSEUM, located in Rosenberg, Texas.

As the reader begins riding through the pages of his early life, several unexpected events will be shared that helped mold young Larry Callies into a "real" cowboy. Cowboy Larry's life-long trail ride begins in Wharton County as he quickly takes hold of the skills and rugged attitudes from his relatives handed down from generations of black cowboys of the Old West.

These early life-lessons will also reveal how his journey to become a cowboy eventually leads him into a brief, but promising professional singing career; and eventually, guides him to open a museum sharing the "hidden history" of the black cowboy.

Texas State Historical Association, Public domain, via Wikimedia Commons

When I was in the third grade, it was picture day when we were told to dress up. I wore a red with white trim cowboy shirt that my mama had bought for me. My mama had earlier bought me a pair of red cowboy boots. With my red boots and red with white trim cowboy shirt, I was fully dressed as a cowboy.

Born in El Campo, Texas, in 1952, Cowboy Larry's story resonates with his song that, "I am Christian first and a cowboy second." As we continue down that dusty trail of hope and promise, it will become apparent that Cowboy Larry had strong influences on his life by his cowboy father and his Christian mother. Unshakable grit, unrelenting compassion, unbending stubbornness, and unmistakable kindness have been the brands of Cowboy Larry to the surprise of friend and foe alike growing up in the segregated, Southeast Texas.

HERE COMES COWBOY LARRY—"STEPPING OUT ON FAITH", is a story told by Larry Callies in his own words to share how dreams can become a reality even when they are faced with impossible odds.

The stories in this book are written in the same language and expressions shared by Cowboy Larry.

In writing this book in this manner, it is our hope that a truer picture of a hard - working, committed cowboy with a deep CHRISTIAN FAITH will be seen.

When I was in the 5th grade, my teacher asked the class what they wanted to be when they grew up. Some said doctors, lawyers, and others said teachers. When I was asked, I said I wanted to be a cowboy.

The class laughed when I said this and my teacher got mad at me because she thought I was trying to be funny. But I didn't mind, my dream was really to be a cowboy!

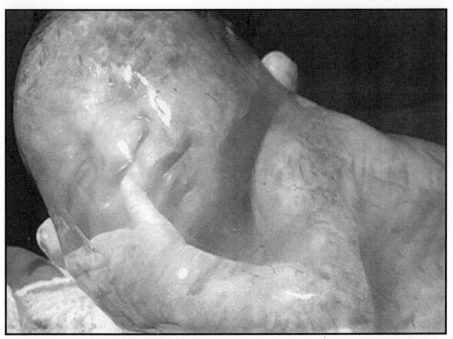

A person born with a "veil over their face" is also called a "Caulbearer" and there is less than 1 in every 80,000 babies born with a veil.

Black cotton farming.

Larry Callies in grade school.

— CHAPTER 1 —

I WAS BORN WITH
A VEIL OVER MY FACE

Hi, my name is Larry Callies and I have a story to tell. I was born on November 12, 1952, in El Campo, Texas. I did not know, but at the time of my birth, I was born with a "veil" over my face.

("Veil" --It is being born with a layer of skin over the face which doctors can surgically remove. A person born with a "veil over their face" is also called a "Caulbearer" and there is a saying that "Caulbearers" are often found to have psychic abilities and believed to be the mark for something special. With less than 1 in every 80,000 babies born with a veil, it comes to no surprise that superstitions and stories surround this mysterious and rare phenomenon." www.quora.com/What-does-the-expression-born-with-a-veil-mean)

This was told to me about 10 years later by my dad, Leon Callies, who told me that I was special because of the "veil". My dad had shared with me that as a toddler, I had seen people coming in our house. He told me he did not see anyone walking in. But I did. That's when he told me I was special. However, my mother, Inell Callies, did not agree with my dad and would often tell me that I was not born special because of the "veil". She told me that was just an old wives' tale.

I was three years old at the time. We had been working on the farm with my grandpa in Blue Creek right outside of El Campo, Texas. My grandpa was in charge of the farm, the tractors, the corn, and cotton fields. I was proud because he owned his fields. He was the only black man at that time that did this. His name was Nathan Callies.

I remembered that on Sunday, my grandpa would wear his special pair of cowboy boots as he went to church. That was when I really wanted to have my own pair of boots. (These boots are now in THE BLACK COWBOY MUSEUM). My grandpa was not a big man, about 5'7" or 5' 8"; but he married a woman who was bigger than he was. We called her "Big Mama."

To my recollection, seeing spirits did not happen for me again until I was 12 years of age. I was attending my aunt's church in El Campo, Texas, when this certain preacher started preaching. I called him a "certain preacher" because he was different from anyone I had known at the time. I would see this "certain preacher" walking down the streets talking to himself and answering himself with all kinds of body movements. Everyone believed he was homeless and a bit "cuckoo." But somehow, he became a preacher.

On that Sunday, he was in my aunt's church preaching. This is the second time I saw spirits. While the preacher was preaching, I saw spirits flying all around the church's ceiling. This was the second time I saw spirits. With the preaching, the shouting, the music, and the spirits flying, I was so scared when I saw and heard this because I had never experienced anything like this before. I really did not know what was going on. I never wanted to go back to church, but my mom "made me" go back to church until I was 17 years old.

My daddy was a rancher and a farmer. During the winter months, he tended cattle. And during the spring and summer months, he grew cotton and corn as a farmer. My mother's name was Inell Callies. She was a housewife taking care of the family.

I had three brothers and a sister. Out of all my brothers and sister, Marvin, Andrew, Leon, and sister, Valerie, I was the only one to come out as a cowboy. I have always wanted to be a cowboy.

When I was in the third grade, it was picture day when you were supposed to dress up and I wore a cowboy shirt that my mom bought for me. It was red with a white trim. Then when I was in the fifth grade, my teacher asked the class what they wanted to be when they grew up. Most of the class responded by saying they wanted to be a doctor, lawyer, teacher. I believe they gave those answers because that is what the teacher expected them to say. I said, "I WANT TO BE A COWBOY!" That is when the class started laughing and that made me smile. The teacher thought I smiled because I was trying to be funny. But I just thought that it was kind of cool. The teacher called me up and gave me a hard spanking because she thought I was trying to be funny. That did not change my mind one bit.

In the first and second grades, my aunt Roberta Callies, was my teacher in a one room schoolhouse. Also, when I was in school, my brother, Marvin, who was in the third grade; my cousin, Morgan Williams, in the third grade; my cousin, Margie Dean, in the first grade with me; and Carolyn Edwards, my first girlfriend crush. My aunt had high expectations for me because she was a Callies and I was a Callies. And because they were kinfolks, my cousins also expected me to do well in school. The more the teacher tried to push me, the less I got it.

In the third grade, I had to go to a larger school in El Campo, Texas where we had at least 20 people in the classroom. In that school, the teachers did not know I had a learning disability; they just thought I was dumb. (This was back in the late 1950's and early 1960's, if you could not learn in the classroom, the teacher considered you were dumb. Many teachers at that time had not received the training to determine learning disabilities such as dyslexia.)

There was another time when a teacher told me to read in the classroom and the students in the classroom started to laugh because they knew I did not like to read out aloud. She came to

My daddy put me on a horse when I was three years old. When I was around 9 or 10 years old, I would go with my daddy to tend the cattle. I did this mainly to keep out of the cotton fields.

I would have to fill one of those long sacks with cotton which would take me the entire summer to do. And at the end, I believed I only received $5.00 for all that work.

My brothers continued to work in the fields. Larry, far right, is pictured with his two brothers playing in the snow.

Black family picking cotton.

my desk and told me I will give you an "F" if you do not read. I told her to give me an "F". That is when the kids stopped laughing and knew it was serious.

This was the beginning of the stubbornness and grit I later became known for. No matter the threat, if I decided to do something or not to do it, I would make sure people knew I stood on my word. The teacher never asked me to read aloud again.

My daddy put me on a horse when I was three years old. When I was around 9 or 10 years old, I would go with my daddy to tend the cattle. I did this mainly to keep out of the cotton fields. I would have to fill one of those long sacks with cotton which would take me the entire summer to do. And at the end, I believed I only received $5.00 for all that work.

Without saying, I did not want to work in the cotton fields. I worked my way out of the cotton fields by being a good horseman. I found out later that is how slaves also got out of working in the cotton fields.

— CHAPTER 2 —

MY ADVENTURE WITH "LIGHTNING AND SMITTY" NEAR THE SAN BERNARD RIVER

When I was 12 years old, Sloan Williams, a cattle rancher in Wharton County, TX, bought a horse that was too old to ride, except for me. I did not have a saddle nor a bridle for the horse, but I found two hay strings and I made my own halter and bridle. The horse was so old, that Sloan was planning to put the horse out to pasture. I asked Sloan if I could ride the old horse. He said I could have the horse. I was so excited because this was my first horse. And this is when I first became a cowboy.

I had to ride the horse with a burlap sack as a blanket on his back. I would jump on that horse and kick him on his sides to run, but he would only walk slowly. He was so poor, when I kicked him on his sides, I could feel his ribs. I named the horse "Lightning" because of the 1950's show, AMOS & ANDY. They had a character on the show who was so slow, they called him, "Lightning."

I rode "Lightning" for two weeks after I came home from school. I continued to try to get lightning to trot or lope, but I could not get him to do either. Then, one day on a Saturday, I was going to the San Bernard River which was about a half mile from our house. I got on "Lightning" and we started walking down to the river with my faithful dog, "Smitty."

I want to tell you a little story about my dog, "Smitty." "Smitty" got his name from my cousin, Calvin Greely, who had been living with us in Hungerford, Texas, for about six months. Cousin Calvin would have been the world champion calf roper but because he was black, he was not allowed to compete in the white rodeos in the early 1960's. Calvin would sometimes come home late at night when everybody was asleep. My dog would be hiding underneath our house when Calvin came home late at night and would jump out and try to bite him. Calvin asked whose dog was this and what was his name. I told Cousin Calvin that it was my dog and I had him for about a year, but I had never given him a name. Then Calvin said, "Let's call him "Smitty." I said okay, and we started calling my dog, "Smitty." So, when Calvin continued to come home late at night, he would call out to "Smitty." "Smitty" got used to Cousin Calvin and stopped trying to bite him.

Now back to the adventure with "Lightning" and "Smitty." It was in the wintertime, but it was not cold. The leaves had fallen from the trees and it was so quiet, I could hear "Lightning" walking on the leaves. We were about ten yards from the river when; suddenly, out of nowhere, I heard this tremendous roar that sent chills down my spine. "Lightning" reared up, turned around, and took off running as fast as lightning! My faithful dog, "Smitty," had already sprinted 20 yards before "Lightning" had even started running. But just in a few seconds, "Lightning" overtook "Smitty," who was running back toward our house. I never dreamed that "Lightning" could run so fast. I was holding on to him for my dear life!

So, when we got back to the house, I saw that "Smitty" had run under the house. I did not see him for several hours after that. "Lightning" had run so fast that he was dripping with sweat. But I really do not know if it was his sweat or that I had "wet" on myself. After that adventure, "Lightning" went back to just walking when I got on him to ride. No matter what I did, I could never get him to run again. About two months later, "Lightning" died, and we had to bury him in the field.

About three or four years later after his death, while looking at a western on television, I heard that same roar that scared me on that faithful day. I said, "That was the sound I heard at the San Bernard River that day. My dad told me that was the sound of a panther. I realized then that it must have been a panther that gave that roar that scared my horse, "Lightning," my faithful dog, "Smitty", and me. It took me a long time before I could ride in the woods by myself after that adventure.

— CHAPTER 3 —

THE STORY ABOUT WHEN MY BROTHER, MARVIN, AND I WERE PENNING BULLS FOR A RODEO IN WHARTON, TEXAS

Back in the early 1960's, my dad, Leon Callies, asked my oldest brother, Marvin, and I to help at a rodeo which was coming to Wharton, Texas. He asked us to pen the bulls that the cowboys would be trying to ride in a rodeo competition.

These bulls had the reputation of the being the best in Texas, probably, the best in the entire world. I was around 12 or 13 when I started penning bulls for rodeos with my oldest brother, Marvin. At this rodeo, we would be penning the meanest and roughest bulls in Texas. Along with Marvin and I, we had help from a friend named, Mingo Sanchez.

My dad was driving trucks at the time we were penning bulls and he said he would not be able to be there. That is when he asked my brother and I to help pen the bulls for the rodeo. We had penned bulls 25 or 30 times before, so we knew what we were doing.

At this rodeo, there was this one bull named, "Wooly Bully." He was named "Wooly Bully" because of his long hair that covered most of his body. This was a Scottish Highlander bull from Scotland.

When we got this bull, he was the meanest bull I had ever seen. My dad had warned me about how mean this bull was and told me to be careful.

When we were unloading him to the pen, I could see him staring at us through the trailer bars. Then, without any warning, he would charge right at us like he wanted to get us. "Wooly Bully" looked like a big grizzly bear with horns. You could not see his eyes, but you knew he could see you. He still looked so mean with the expression on the rest of his face with his snorting and grunting that bulls make like you see in a bull fight. I could tell that the other bulls were afraid of him too as we unloaded him off the truck and they distanced themselves away from him. Anyone would come to the same conclusion that if he did not have the horns, he would look like a bear because his hair covered this whole body all the way to the ground.

The cowboys were also scared of "Wooly Bully." And when they found out that he could buck, they really did not want to ride him. At the rodeo, the cowboys soon began calling the bull, "The Beatle", because around 1964, the owner of the bull, Sloan Williams, started calling him, "The Beatle," after the famous rock group, "The Beatles." When cowboys tried to ride him, they would play the song, "Wooly Bully" and the crowd loved it.

There was this bull that was given the name, "The Beatle," by his owner, Sloan Williams. The Beatle was a Scottish bull covered with long hair and had a reputation of stomping and hooking its riders.

Another thing about this bull was that he was very quick and mean that when the cowboys fell off him, he would soon turn and hook them. His horns were so sharp, that we had to tip them because he was hurting a lot of cowboys. And "The Beatle" was not finished when he bucked the cowboys off him. He would then go after the clowns. They were scared to death of him! After a year or so after hooking many cowboys and going after the clowns hurting them too, I could tell from what he would do each time he was being rode, that he figured out what he was there for—to entertain the people.

"The Beatle" would go through his motion of kicking up his legs, pawing the ground throwing sand over his back and creating a cloud of dust; snorting and grunting like the bulls in a bull fighting ring. Then, all you could see was a bunch of hair in a cloud of dust when the cowboys rode him.

I loved to watch it and the crowd did too! This was "The Beatle's" routine performance as he came out of the shoot with a cowboy on his back hearing each time the roar and applause of the rodeo crowd.

After many rodeo appearances, I soon noticed that "The Beatle" stopped hooking the cowboys after he bucked them off his back and hurting the clowns. He would buck the cowboys off first and then would go straight after the clowns.

I noticed on several occasions when the bull could have easily hurt a cowboy or a clown as he had done before; but now, he would just buck the cowboy off and then charge at both of them like he was going to hurt them. Instead of hurting the cowboy or the clown, "The Beatle" would quickly turn to the side and miss them; but then, shook his head as if to say, "You can't ride me!".

After a year and a half after penning the bull, I could even pet "The Beatle" through the trailer bars. This would also happen at rodeos where "The Beatle" performed. When he went out in the rodeo arena, he acted like the meanest bull in the world; but when he came back to go in the shoot, he would not try to hurt anyone.

The thing I learned from watching "The Beatle" was that bulls can think for themselves. And how I know this to be true was that on another occasion later in the 1960's, I saw another bull do the same thing I saw "The Beatle" do. I saw another bull do a clown act where he appeared to be running the clown down to really hurt him; but when the clown fell to the ground, the bull turned aside, shook his head, and didn't even try to hook or step on him. I concluded that this bull and the clown were doing a "clown act"! The response of the people was their roaring applause of approval. Like the clown, the bull knew exactly what the people wanted him to do—to entertain them.

I also remember, "back in the day," I saw this rodeo clown named, "Ralph Fisher" take a Brahma bull and put him in a one-horse trailer to go to a rodeo in Katy, Texas. Ralph had worked with this bull before and had witnessed over the years that when he would buck off a cowboy, instead of hooking him, this bull would charge at the cowboy and then stop, start shaking his head, and would let the cowboy run out of the arena.

One day when this same bull had bucked off the cowboy, he started charging Ralph the clown. As Ralph was running to escape the charging bull, he fell to the ground. But instead of stepping on him or hooking Ralph, this same bull immediately stopped in his tracks, shook his head, and did not hook or step on Ralph. Ralph immediately saw that this was an entertaining act that the crowd loved!

Ralph then bought this white, Brahma bull so that he could perform this same act in future rodeos, which he did. When Ralph got to a rodeo, he would unload the bull into the pen. When it was time for them to come into the arena, the bull

Ralph Fisher, famous rodeo clown with Oscar — the bull fighting buzzard, entertained rodeo crowds across the USA.

would come out looking mean—snorting, grunting, and kicking up dust. Then he would start chasing Ralph the clown around the arena. Suddenly, Ralph would fall to the ground and the crowd would become fearful that the bull was going to step on him or hook him. But to their amazement, the bull would stop in his tracks, shake his head, and would not hurt a hair on the head of the clown. The crowd gave a thunderous roar of applause. Then Ralph the clown would get up, start running again; the bull would start chasing him again, and he would trip and fall. The act was complete when the bull would stop in his tracks, shake his head, and the crowd gave its expected applause of approval for both the bull and the clown.

"The thing I learned from watching "The Beatle" was that bulls can think for themselves."

— CHAPTER 4 —

THE TALE OF TWO BULLS
V61 (OR SLIM JIM) AND 2 WHITE LIGHTNING

Marvin, Mingo, and I were penning bulls for a rodeo in Crosby, Texas, when I noticed a bull, "V61," who we called "Slim Jim," was the first bull leading the herd. This was strange to me because for 30 times I had penned the bulls before, "Slim Jim" was always the last bull in the herd to be penned.

The reason for "Slim Jim" staying at the end of the herd was that he did not want any part of a bull we called, "2 White Lightning," who normally stayed behind the herd to be penned, had been bullying and fighting him many times before.

On this day, "Slim Jim" was in the front of the herd as if he were waiting for something. After a few of the bulls came through the pen, "2 White Lightning" approached the front of the pen. And just as soon as he got to where "Slim Jim" was, "Slim Jim" rammed "2 White Lightning" as hard as he could and knocked him to the ground. Stunned, "2 White Lightning" quickly got up looking for the bull, "Slim Jim," who had rammed him and had immediately took off running. You could tell that "2 White Lightning" was mad and started chasing "Slim Jim" who by this time, had ran inside to the far side of the pen. Then, as "2 White Lightning" entered the pen to get "Slim Jim," "Slim Jim" ran out of a different gate to the practice pen. I saw "2 White Lightning" chasing "Slim Jim" and closed the gate behind "Slim Jim" so that "2 White Lightning" could not get to him. You could tell "2 White Lightning" was still mad as he tried to get to "Slim Jim," but he could not. From that day forward when we were hauling the bulls, we had to put "Slim Jim" in the front of the truck and 2 White Lighting in the back of the truck.

That night at the Crosby rodeo, "2 White Lightning" came out of the shoot bucking as hard as he ever had. He was one of Sloan Williams' best bucking bulls and he was proving it that night. As I watched "2 White Lightning" bucking, hurling, and twisting his huge body through the air, I could also see "Slim Jim" out of the corner of my eye watching what "2 White Lightning" was doing. "Slim Jim" was getting agitated. And when it was "Slim Jim's" turn to be ridden, he came out of the shoot bucking harder than he ever bucked before. That's when the cowboy flew so high in the air, the crowd was amazed to see a cowboy thrown off a bull that high. "Slim Jim" had been ridden by cowboys for three or four months and had never bucked a cowboy off him before. On that night, "Slim Jim" became Sloan Williams' best bucking bull.

In 1970, the National Finals Rodeo voted V61, or "Slim Jim," to be the "bull of the year." V61 was later featured in a story in Life Magazine. "Slim Jim" also made the HALL OF FAME FOR RODEO BULLS. This bull would first jump out of the shoot and it would be near 20 feet in the air. He kind of kept his hind feet under his body like a bronc when he jumped; and then, when he

2 White Lightning was a large brahma bull that had a reputation of being the meanest bull for cowboys to ride, and a bull that would truly "bully" other bulls in the pen.

hit the ground, he would kick them out. That is when you really felt the power—when he hit the ground. He had the power to pull a cowboy down on his head. It was believed that this bull could learn how cowboys would try to ride him and would use that knowledge to buck them off. If the cowboy were right-handed, he would buck and twist to the left; and if the cowboy were left-handed, he would buck and twist to the right, bucking them off each time. V61 had been bucked out 250 times before a cowboy could finally ride him for 8 seconds.

One day, while sitting in a barn, me and my brothers, Marvin, and Andrew, heard this loud commotion that was happening outside in the pasture. We looked through the barn window and we saw several bulls fighting. We immediately thought that it was "2 White Lightning" who had started the fighting because he had been the one starting the fights before.

But to our surprise, we saw five bulls ganging up on "2 White Lightning." We saw these bulls taking turns charging and ramming him with their horns. As they moved closer to the barbed-wire fence, about 50 yards from it, they started surrounding "2 White Lightning". As the group of bulls moved closer to the fence with "2 White Lightning" in the center, they charged him and lifted "2 White Lightning" and threw him over that barbed-wire fence! This was a sight to see.

Then we saw "2 White Lightning," who was fighting mad, trying to get back to where the other bulls were on the other side of the barbed-wire fence. As hard as he tried, "2 White Lightning" could not cross the barrier of the barbed-wire fence. That is when my brothers and I got some horses to guide "2 White Lightning" into a special pen. From that day forward, we had to keep "2 White Lightning" separated from the other bulls in his own pen.

Another reason we had to separate "2 White Lightning" was that he really was a bully. He was not that big of a Brahma bull, but he was tough. Big or small, "2 White Lightning" would challenge any bull in the pen. Many of the bulls would turn and run; and when they did, he would charge them and he would hook them in the butt with his horns. But those who would stand their ground and fight, "2 White Lightning" would fight them if it took all day until he won.

V61 (c. 1962 – 1974) was one of the best bulls Sloan Williams of Wharton County, Texas, owned before he was sold to a rodeo company.

Larry Callies and his brother, Marvin, used to pen V61 in rodeos in Southeast Texas.

"Puggy" (Leon Callies, Larry's daddy) herded the cows back from the woods that Larry and the dogs had just chased out of the woods.

— CHAPTER 5 —

WHEN GOD SAVED MY LIFE
AND I DIDN'T KNOW HE KNEW MY NAME

There are strange events in a person's life that cannot easily be explained. It can be said that this one event fits this description which happened to me one day when I was 12 years old working cows with my dad in Hungerford, Texas.

We were working cows one day and we saw three cows off in the woods on the other side of the thicket in a clearing. We stayed on our horses for about 10 – 15 minutes looking for the dogs to bring them out. But we could not find a way to get in or get them out. Next thing I know, my dad turned to me and told me that I had to go in the thicket to get those cows out of there.

Those three cows were about 40 yards from us in a thicket where only cows and dogs could get in. Looking a little closer, I saw a trail that had been covered by sticker bushes just wide enough for cows with an opening they must have made going in the woods. Only someone small could get into that opening.

As I looked at the opening and the trail, I told my dad that I was scared to go in there to get those cows. My day told me, "Boy, go on in there and get them cows."

Knowing that my dad meant what he said that he wanted me to go in there to get the cows out, I started slowly making my way down the trail when I felt the ground started shaking and I heard the loud sounds of cows mooing and dogs barking coming straight at me. My dad had told me earlier to get some rocks and sticks to throw at the cows to get them moving out of the woods; but at that moment, I really did not need them. (I found out later in life that slaves used sticks and rocks in the 1850's and 60's to get cows out of the woods.) I could tell that they were about 20 yards away from running me down.

At that moment, I could hear the cows mooing and the dogs barking. I was really scared. Just when the first cow was about to run over me, I looked up and saw a low hanging branch. I jumped up, grabbed it, and hung on for dear life as the first cow came thundering right under me. The branch lifted me high enough that only my hanging feet ran across the cow's back as she ran down the trail.

A couple of seconds later and there was the second cow steaming down the trail, mowing down weeds and stickers, kicking up clops of dirt and grass as I struggled to hold on to a tree branch that seem to come out of nowhere. This cow was running so fast that she did not pay me any mind. Besides the noise from the cows and the dogs, adding to my fear was the branch I was hanging on to started giving way to my weight. Then both of my knees and feet were hanging so low that they grazed the back of the cow that thundered right under me.

Finally, a few seconds later, and the third cow came plowing through that same narrow pass that the other two had come just missing me as I hung from my miracle branch. But this time, the third cow was not alone as it was the dogs nipping at the hind feet of the cows that had started them stampeding back towards me. By this time, the branch was about to give way to my weight that I was so low, when the cow came running fearful of the barking dogs, she hit me in my stomach knocking the wind out of me. I went to the ground trying to breathe but I could not because the wind had been knocked out of me by the cow. I really thought that this was it for me. But it was not! My miracle branch had held me long enough for the cows and the dogs to pass.

The cows and the dogs came out of the opening of the trail where my dad was waiting on his horse. Lying on the ground, I then heard a shout from my dad, "Larry?" I knew my dad wanted me to answer him, but I could not because the wind had been knocked out of me. My dad cried out a second time but much louder, "Larry!" Again, I wanted to answer for I was still gasping for air. And with an even louder shout, my dad called out my name again, "Larry?" By then, I had walked out the thicket. My dad said, "Boy, why didn't you answer me?" Now, by that time, I was able to breathe. I told my dad that I could not answer him because the wind was knocked out of me. He then said, "Larry, are you okay?" But before I could answer, I saw for the first time tears welled up in my dad's eyes.

I had never seen this before because my dad was a big man. He had a build like the heavyweight boxer, Ken Norton. In fact, my dad had won the golden gloves in the heavyweight division and held that title for a couple of years in Wharton county. He was known as being the best cowboy, probably in the whole state of Texas. He was especially known for his skill in calf-roping. He was tough; a "real cowboy—the best!" And I am proud to say I learned from the best!

He helped me up and we walked to where the horses were. The last thing I remember that day was as we sat on our horses; I saw my dad wipe away a tear again. I believe he had been fearful that his son had been injured or even killed by those stampeding cows. We then had a good time rounding up those cows and getting them back to the herd.

As I remember this day when I was a young boy, I cannot help but believe that God saved my life that day. I really did not know God at the time or have a close relationship with him then, but I believed He knew my name and was watching over me. Looking back, I believe He has been watching over me my entire life.

"Looking back,
I believe He has been
watching over me
my entire life."

— CHAPTER 6 —

WADING IN THE WATER
THE DAY I GOT BAPTIZED
IN THE "BLUE HOLE"

I was in Hungerford, Texas, at my mother's church with my brothers during a Summer Revival. Reverend Winchester was the preacher for the three-day revival. Each night, Reverend Winchester would ask at the end of his preaching, "Who would like to give their life to Christ?" That night before we went to the revival, my mother asked me and my brothers if any of us wanted to give our lives to Jesus Christ. My mama, Mrs. Inell Callies, was a faithful Christian woman. She never missed going to church and she made sure my brothers, sister, and I went. And she did not believe in being late going to church. I often saw her reading her bible and praying. And I can also say, she strongly believed in what the bible taught about chastising children when they have done something wrong! My mama had a great influence on me becoming a Christian to where it became first in my life; and being a cowboy, became second. But on that day, during that hot summer of the revival, I told her that I was not going to do it. I did not want to give my life to Christ. I was the only one of my brothers who spoke up.

As the preaching came to an end that night, Reverend Winchester asked if anyone wanted to come up and give their life to Christ. I was seated next to my brothers. My best friend, Giaroud Howe, was seated at the end of the pew. I was totally surprised when during the invitation to become a Christian, I saw my friend slowly get up and start walking toward the preacher. I said in my mind, "I wasn't going to do that!" But then, just a few seconds later, I had a strange sensation come over me and I found myself standing up and walking toward the preacher too. And that is when I gave my life to Jesus Christ. I was 15 years old when I did this and then got baptized the next Sunday, in Kendleton, Texas.

The whole church went to the San Bernard River for baptizing new Christians which was close to where "Madam Powell" had her stagecoach depot during the time of the Texas Revolutionary War against Mexico. We went to a place in the river known as the "Blue Hole." It had a reputation of being so deep that no one could ever touch the bottom. It was also the place where everyone went to be baptized because it was said to have "healing powers."

My whole family was there when I got baptized. We all wore white sheets as Reverend Winchester took us in the river one by one. There were 10 people to go "wading in the water" that day. I was scared when I got baptized as a young boy because we were being baptized in a river and I could not swim.

The preacher did not tell me to hold my breath or pinch my nose tight to keep from swallowing water when he would lower me under the water to be baptized.

Next, as he placed his hand over my face, I heard these words; "I now baptize Larry Callies in the name of the Father, the Son, and the Holy Ghost…!" I was then dunked under the water by the preacher for about three seconds and brought up quickly gasping for air and spitting out water.

I got a mouth full of water and water up my nose! I then heard a lot of "Amens" and "Thank you Jesus" and singing coming from the church folk as I was now baptized.

The revival took place at my mama's home church, Mt. Scilla Baptist Church, in Hungerford, Texas.

The very next Sunday, the entire church went to Kendleton, Texas, to the East Bernard River or the "Blue Hole" for my baptism along with nine other people. My whole family came to see my baptism.

(Picture Courtesy of LIPSTICKALLEY.COM)

Damien Krushal, present day champion young bull rider from Wharton, Texas, is pictured riding a steer similar to what Larry Callies rode at the age of 15 in Simonton, Texas.

— CHAPTER 7 —

MY FIRST RODEO,
RIDING A STEER IN SIMONTON, TEXAS

I rode my first steer when I was 15 years old in Simonton, Texas, on November 9, 1968. My dad was furnishing the stock for this Black Cowboy Rodeo. I had told my mama that I wanted to get in the steer riding competition, and she told me that she would come. This was the first time my mama came to see me ride.

Like in many Black Cowboy Rodeos in Southeast Texas, this was also a time for blues singers to come and provide extra entertainment. The Blues singer, Bobby Blue Bland, happened to be at this rodeo in Simonton, Texas, that night.

Everyone was getting bucked off their steers that night. But when it came to me, I was able to ride my steer the full 8 seconds and I won the steer riding championship.

After my ride, Bobby Blue Bland called me over to the stands and said, "Boy, come over here. I want to shake your hand!" I was proud of myself because I not only won the steer riding championship, I also got to shake hands with the famous blues singer, Bobby Blue Bland. I also got some praise from my mama when she said, "Boy, you did good!"

During the days of segregation when Black Cowboys could not participate in all white rodeos, black communities often had their own rodeos in small towns and country venues which featured opening parades, "the cowboy's prayer", gospel quartets and blues singers, and the trademark barbeque and fish sandwiches always with bragging rights.

The Black Rodeos usually had packed crowds. During the late 1960's, that was the place to be to see Black Cowboys ride and Blues Singers sing. That was the place to go, and it was the thing to do. This was a good rodeo too because Tex Williams, my cousin, won the saddle bronc riding competition.

There were other local famous or soon to be famous black cowboys at this rodeo in 1968. They were: Willie Thomas; Clint Wyche; James Thomas; my cousin, Sonny Cook; my cousin Calvin Greely; and Scott Green.

These are the Champion Cowboys of the Rodeo in Simonton, Texas, in 1968 at my first rodeo competition as a teenager. Three of the cowboys were my cousins: Calvin Greely, Tex Williams, and Sonny Cook.

I was not in the picture because the other cowboys all won money, but I only won a trophy.

Pictured is the Juneteenth Celebration held in Macbeth, Texas, where "bulldogging" was an event at the rodeo.

Larry Callies was in attendance and he was 15 years old at the time. Bulldogging the steer is Calvin Greely. Calvin could have been the first black World Champion "calf-roper" in the 1960's and 70's; but they wouldn't let him win because he was black.

As I watched them participate at this rodeo, I had a sketchy remembrance of my very first rodeo as a toddler of three years old. I remembered my very first rodeo was in Egypt, Texas, during a Juneteenth Celebration in 1955. I remember standing up in my dad's old pick-up truck watching my daddy, uncles, and cousins compete in the all black cowboy rodeo of that day.

It is funny, but I can also remember that it was extremely hot that day and I was drinking red soda water and eating cold watermelon while watching them. I really liked that; it was the thing to do back then.

> "I also got some praise from my mama when she said, "Boy, you did good!"

— CHAPTER 8 —

THE FIRST COMPETITION, RIDING A BULL I KNEW I COULDN'T RIDE

When I started riding in rodeo competition at WHARTON COUNTY JUNIOR COLLEGE, I drew a bull I knew I could not ride. I had seen this bull buck before, and it was one of Sloan Williams' stock bulls.

I was the person who hauled Sloan Williams' bulls to the rodeos at WHARTON COUNTY JUNIOR COLLEGE. There was this certain banana horned bull that was really a tough bull to ride. And this was the bull I drew in my first rodeo competition and I knew I could not ride it.

I didn't want people to think I was scared to ride this bull, so when the crowd was looking at another bull rider come out of the shoot with a bull before me, I went down on my knees and prayed. The crowd could not see me praying because I was out of plain sight down in a shoot when I prayed. I knew that this bull was quick and would spin so I prayed a prayer not to win this competition, but that God would keep me safe.

When I got on the bull, he jumped out of the shoot to the left. This was good for me because I rode left-handed. But just as quickly he jumped to the left, the bull then started jumping and spinning to the right. After about three or four seconds, I hit hard on the ground and landed on my butt. I found myself sitting on the arena ground with my hands to my side praying again that God would not let this bull step on my fingers or body. Within a short time, this bull had jumped four or five times over me as I sat on the ground and then something hit me across my face. The force of whatever hit me knocked me face down to the ground. The next thing I remembered was I saw the bull that had just bucked me off heading toward the "let out-shoot." I then jumped up, ran to my buddy, Willie Sanders, who was like a rodeo clown in the arena, and asked him, what was it that hit me in my face? He told me he did not know what hit me.

I explained to him that whatever it was, that it felt like someone smack me in the face real hard with a pillow. Again, my friend said he did not see anything hit me in the face. So, as I went over to get my bull rope, I went over to the back pen to look at the bull that had just bucked me off. And that is when I noticed that this bull had "extra-long nuts". That's when I realized that it must have been those "extra-long nuts" of the bull that had hit me in the face as I was in the middle of the rodeo arena. God had answered my prayer, the bull did not step on my fingers, nor hit my body.

A few years later as I remembered this first bull that I rode in a rodeo competition, I also realized that God must have a sense of humor. What I prayed for that God would keep me safe and not allow that bull to step on my fingers or hurt me, that prayer was answered; but I knew God had to have been watching over me as only that bull's "nuts" was the only thing that touched me.

Larry Callies rode bulls, roped calves, and was a team steer roper.

Larry practiced roping steers on a ranch in Hungerford, TX, in preparation to compete in local rodeos.

— CHAPTER 9 —

WHAT I LEARNED FROM MY DAD, LEON CALLIES, ALSO KNOWN AS "PUGGY"

When I think about my dad, a big smile comes across my face because I had a lot of great times with him. I admired my dad. He was my hero. My dad was a cowboy; and I wanted to be just like him. He was the greatest cowboy I have ever known, and I learned a lot from him. Sometimes, my memories take me back in time and I can see my dad sitting tall in the saddle as he did so many times when we rode together.

To begin with, I had three brothers and one sister and there was no doubt in our house as to who was the head of it. When my dad told us to do something, there was no back talk nor any slacking around to do the job. He was a man of tall stature and well-built like a professional boxer. Many people had said that he resembled Ken Norton, a one-time, Heavy-weight Boxing Champion of the World.

When he entered a room, his presence demanded attention and respect. Sometimes he would call my brothers and say, "Boy," to get our immediate attention and I knew then this meant we had to do something and do it then. Other times, he would call us by name, "Larry," which seemed to be a stern request to get something done in a timely manner. He rarely repeated himself when telling any of us to do things because we knew we had better listen the first time.

We usually ate all three meals together as a family except when we were in school. My mother was an excellent cook and she made some homemade rolls that did not take a back seat to anyone.

My dad assigned all his children chores teaching us the value of being timely and taking care of responsibilities. In all my years with him, my dad was never late for a job or an appointment. To be on time was especially important to him and this was easy for me to learn because he always practiced it. He also wanted us to learn the value of working for what you want in life.

My oldest brother, Marvin, and I had the responsibility of milking the cows every morning. He also taught us how to pick and chop cotton which we all had to do in Wharton, Texas. Hauling hay was hard work but it was also kind of fun to me because that is when I learned how to drive a standard shift truck.

When I was about 10 or 11, my dad taught me how to handle the clutch and the brakes and to keep the truck in a straight line as he would work the bales of hay and throw them on the back of the truck. Driving out in the hay fields is exactly where I learned not only how to drive a standard shift truck, but to gain confidence in myself once I learned something. To this day, the standard shift truck is my preferred truck to drive.

My dad was the lead cowboy on Sloan Williams' ranch in charge of many farm and ranch hands. Taking care of the stock on the ranch was an important job which my dad taught to my brother, Marvin, and me.

We were taught how to load and unload bulls that were taken to area rodeos which we often did to help my dad when he sometimes drove a truck far out of town deliveries. My dad was a great provider for our family, wearing many hats in doing so.

"Puggy" was the name my dad's friends and our kinfolks would call him. He would usually take me along with him when he tended the stock or check on my older brothers and the other ranch hands working in the cotton fields and with the stock. People started calling me, "Little Puggy," because I usually rode by my dad's side and would always try to imitate what he was doing.

It is amazing that I can even remember when my dad placed me on a horse. I was around three years old and I believe it was then that I started dreaming about being a cowboy.

There was a time when we had come back to the house and I saw how my dad was handling a young horse. He warned me to stay away from that horse because he told me that he was "bad." My dad told me not to try and pet this horse because he would quickly try to kick, paw, or even stomp me to death.

Early in my life, because of my dad, I gained a healthy respect of all horses and bulls and became able to identify the ones to watch out for.

I also learned that if you knew how to ride a horse well, you would not have to work in the cotton fields and pick cotton. Fifty years later, as I prepared to open my museum, I discovered that slaves learned to ride horses well to keep themselves from working out in the cotton fields.

It was not long when I was riding alongside my dad all the time, escaping the hard work in the cotton fields. Because I looked like my dad, "Puggy", and I was his constant shadow, people started calling me, "Little Puggy." And even today, I am still called, "Little Puggy," by family and friends.

I had much to be proud of my dad for. The early description of my dad being built like the heavy-weight boxer, Ken Norton, also enabled him to compete in the golden gloves in Wharton County Texas, which he won.

Because he was also lead cowboy on one of the biggest ranches in Wharton, Texas, he became highly skilled as a calf-roper. He was considered to be the best in Texas, and he had the chance to prove it as my cousin, Clarence Gonzalez, and my dad competed in the 1958 World Rodeo Championship in Madison Square Garden in New York. My dad and cousin were among the few black men to compete in a field of over 50 cowboys and my dad won 2nd Place in calf-roping. Calf-roping is another skill my dad taught me which allowed me to win saddles, belt buckles, and prize money in rodeos over the years.

Even though I was born in El Campo, I was raised in Boling, Texas, after we had moved there when I was in the third grade.

Because my dad was also lead cowboy on one of the biggest ranches in Wharton, Texas, he became highly skilled as a calf-roper. He was considered to be the best in Texas. He had the chance to prove it, as my cousin, Clarence Gonzalez, and my dad competed in the 1958 World Rodeo Championship in Madison Square Garden in New York City.

My daddy moved our entire family to Boling, Texas, to work for the largest rancher in Wharton, Texas—Mr. Slone Williams. He was a stock producer who took cattle to area rodeos for competition. I eventually graduated from Boling High School in 1971. While there at the high school, I was the second black to make it to the state rodeo championship finals in bronc riding.

Besides tending the stock and other ranching duties, my father was an expert calf-roper. He was able to participate in calf-roping in some of the small local rodeos and won several of them.

My father learned how to be a cowboy from my uncle who was called BIG PREACHER WILLIAMS, who was from El Campo, Texas. He was known as the "best cowboy" in the country—the best saddle bronc rider without a doubt.

Everybody in this country knew that BIG PREACHER was the best. Those smaller local rodeos where they had jackpots and smaller type awards, he participated in them and won many of them. Back in the 40's, 50's, and 60's, they would not allow black cowboys participate in the organized white, sanctioned rodeos. But in the 1960's, his son, TEX WILLIAMS, proved that he was the best—"the chip off the old block!"

TEX WILLIAMS could participate in the white rodeos beginning in 1967 at the high school level. And while a student at El Campo High School, he won the state rodeo high school championship, Hallettsville, Texas, in 1967 and 1968. He was BIG PREACHER'S son; he was my cousin. Just like my cousin,

And one of the most important lessons my dad taught me was how to deal with people calling me the "n-word."

Tex, learned from his dad, I learned my rodeo skills from my dad. He was the best calf-roper. And I learned from him.

Even though my dad was not a regular church goer like my mama, he taught me some Christian values which I later discovered are found in the Bible. He had great love for my mama, always treating her with the respect and kindness that all women should have. He never came home drunk or stayed out all night or put his hands on her. I saw the gentle side of my dad as he would always open the doors for my mama and even when they had disagreements, there would not be the shouting or the

ALL IN THE FAMILY — "Preacher Williams," (top left) was known as one of the best "real" cowboys in the state of Texas." "Little Preacher Callies", (top right), was also known as one of the best "real" cowboys in state of Texas. He would always follow "Preacher Williams" wherever he went. Bronc busting or bull riding, they excelled in both. They were Larry Callies' uncles. Ike Callis (bottom left), and Laval Callis, (bottom right), were hired cowboys on ranchers in Edna, Texas. They were both Larry Callies' cousins.

ALL IN THE FAMILY — TEX Williams, (top picture), the son of Preacher Williams and cousin of Larry Callies, was the first African American to participate and win the Texas State Rodeo High School Finals in 1967.

Uncle Willie and Roberta Callies, (bottom left). Uncle Willie, a former cowboy from El Campo, Texas, he was a drover on cattle drives from El Campo to Galveston before the trains came to El Campo. Dwight and Lorena Callis (bottom right). Dwight, another cousin, provided Larry with key information about his family's history which guided Larry to the discovery of his ancestry with the Kerr-Mitchell Families. He is the County Extension Agent for the Texas A&M University.

usual slamming of the doors. As I said before, my dad was a great provider for our entire family, especially my mama who did not have to work outside of the home.

And one of the most important lessons my dad taught me was how to get along in a world that is full of hatred and prejudice. He showed me in his dealing with different people that a little kindness will go a long way, even with people who hate you. And he modeled for me the confidence of a proud man who knew who he was, where he came from, and what he was able to do; no matter what people may say or believe.

My dad taught me much more, but these are a few of the most important things that "Puggy", my dad, has taught me which I have carried with me my entire life.

"Calf-roping" was my dad's specialty and it is also mine along with "team-steer roping." I have been blessed to win many cash awards and prizes during my rodeo career.

My dad taught me so much about horses; not only to ride them well, but he taught me how to "read" horses to know their disposition.

My dad also taught me the technique of steer roping which helped me win many rodeo competitions.

— CHAPTER 10 —

MY MAMA, INELL MITCHELL CALLIES, TOLD ME, "LARRY, YOU NEED TO KNOW THAT THERE IS A GOD!"

My mother was a quiet woman. She never wanted to be in the spotlight. She was happy to be the wife of Leon Callies and the mother of her five children, Marvin, Larry, Andrew, Leon, and Valerie. She was mostly a stay at home wife but did some cleaning for Sloan Williams wife. She also picked cotton in the fields with her father in law, Nathan Callies. She cooked us three meals a day or sometimes two, but the lunch meal was enough for us to eat at supper. She was the best Christian person I have ever met. I would see her pray often regardless of who was watching her.

I happened to walk by the door and would see her praying. She told me one day, "Boy, you need to know that there is a God." I told my mother that I don't know who God was or where He was. And I couldn't see how God could be watching everything we do.

My mother was also one of the best cooks in the world. She never drank or smoked. My mother was timely. And she went to church every Sunday unless she was deathly sick. The preacher made an example of her one Sunday. He said, "More people need to be like Sister Callies because she would come to church even when she is sick." She once told me that she lived to go to church. She said, "Boy, I live to go to church." My mother sang in the choir and was an usher standing during most of the Sunday service. She served as an usher until she had diabetes and had to sit in a wheelchair. She even went to church when she had diabetes.

My mother taught me to treat women right, to hold the door open for them and to always treat them kindly. She also told me that money was not everything. I told her that money was and that it made the world go around. She said, "Boy, money doesn't make the world go around; God makes the world go around." Years later, I found out she was right. My mother was the one who did the discipline in the house. She would use a cotton stalk as a switch. And that thing really hurt!

When I left home, I did not go to church for about 15 years except on every Thanksgiving and Christmas. But one day, after I had bought a 1984 Ford Bronco, I called my mother and asked her if she wanted me to take her to church on Sunday. My mother was happy to hear that I was coming to take her to church on Sunday.

That Sunday morning, I came to the house in my brand new, red, and tan, 1984 Ford Bronco; and when she saw it, she turned around and went back into the house. She said, "Boy, I am not going to church with you." I asked her why. She then said, "You just came to show off your new truck." She then stopped, dropped her keys, and thought for a minute. She came back to the door and said, "Boy, I am going to go ahead and go to church with you so you will know whose truck that belongs to." On that day, the preacher never said anything about the truck.

Fast forward twenty years later. I was roping in Rosenberg, Texas, on a Sunday and a preacher named Harvey Abkey was preaching at the rodeo. I was riding on my horse when I heard him say, "Cowboys, do you know that the truck that you are driving ain't your truck? Do you know the trailer you are pulling out there, ain't your trailer? And Cowboys do you know the horse you are riding ain't your horse? Harvey then said, that's God's truck; that's God's trailer; and that's God's horse. When he said that about my truck, I remembered what my mother had said to me years ago that the truck I was driving was not my truck.

He got me when he said that all those things that I believed belonged to me, belonged to God instead. That is when I got interested in knowing who this preacher was. I introduced myself to Harvey Abkey and I asked him if he had a church and where it was. He said it was across the freeway on Bamore Road and he said he had church every Sunday and invited me to come. It was the Bamore Baptist Church of Rosenberg.

I started going to his church and I liked the church so much that I started taking my son, Dylan, to the church. Then my whole family started going to the church with me. One Sunday, Harvey asked me a question, "Didn't you use to sing?" I told him that I did use to sing until I lost my voice. He asked me if I could play bass guitar at the church, and I told him yea. After playing bass at the church for a few months, my son Dylan wanted to play bass guitar too. So, I let him play bass when he was 10 years old. That is when I started playing lead guitar at the church. That was also the best time of my life when I went roping with Harvey at the rodeos.

One day, Harvey asked me where God was. I told him, "God is everywhere." He said, "No, Larry. God is in your heart. He is in everyone's heart." That is when I figured out there was a God, He could see what I was doing, and He could feel what I was feeling because He was inside me. It all made sense. And that is because of God's Son, Jesus Christ, who died on the cross for all men's sins and can come into a person's life and live inside of them.

My mother planted this seed many years ago in my life as I would see her praying, taking us to church, living the Christian life, and telling me about who she knew who God is. And because of that seed she planted and what I leaned with my friend, Harvey Abkey; it has grown within me to where my life's motto is, **"I am a Christian first; and a cowboy second!"**

Larry gives a personal tour of THE BLACK COWBOY MUSEUM whenever visitors come. After he introduces himself, he always begins his oral presentation with the following words, "I am a Christian first and a cowboy second!" He has kept this traditional opening since the opening of his museum which was influenced by his mama.

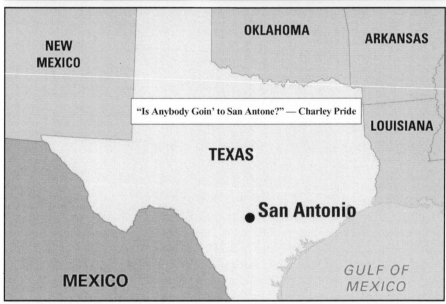

"Is Anybody Goin' to San Antone?" — Charley Pride

NEW MEXICO

OKLAHOMA

ARKANSAS

TEXAS

LOUISIANA

San Antonio

MEXICO

GULF OF MEXICO

— CHAPTER 11 —

THE FIRST TIME I SAW
Charley Pride IN PERSON

My dad and I had a job in Johnson City, Texas. I had some white
friends there and they said that Charley Pride was going to be there
at the rodeo, and they wanted to go see him. They asked me if I
wanted to go hear him and I said, no, because black people were
not supposed to listen to country music. They said why? And I told
them that black people were not supposed to listen to white people's
music. Well, they said Charley Pride is different. And I said, no he is
not. At the time, I did not know that Charley Pride was black.

When they told me that Charley Pride was going to be here, I had
been working some bulls in the back at this rodeo. They said that
later on, he would be here at the rodeo. When I was working the
bulls in the back of the rodeo, I saw a bunch of cops walking this
black man in at the back of the pavilion and I thought he was in
trouble. I saw about six or seven cops surrounding this black guy
and they were walking him into the building. I was wondering,
what did he do. My friend then said, "Larry, Larry, here comes
Charley Pride!" I went up the side of the building. Back in 1968,
they did not have air condition and the windows were up. They
said, "There he goes, Larry." And I said, "Where is he?" They said,
"He is the guy with the microphone." I said, "I saw a black guy
putting a microphone in a microphone stand and I thought it was

for somebody else." They said, "Larry, that's Charley Pride!" I said, "That's Charley Pride?" They said, "Yeah. You didn't know he was black?" "No!" I was mesmerized from that time on. Charley played and I knew every one of his songs.

And then that night, Charley Pride came out at the rodeo and he was in the middle of the arena performing. President Johnson was sitting up in the stands and he was sitting up about twelve feet from where I was working the bulls under the shoot. The President had a sky box right up on top and I said to myself, I see Charley Pride and President Lyndon Johnson right above me. It was pretty cool! I wish I had a camera. I was 16 or 17 at the time. I never thought I would see a President in the flesh. Charley Pride was there performing for the President. He sang all his favorite songs. He sang, "Mountain of "Love," "Kaliyah", "Is Anybody Goin' to San Antone?" That is the true story when I saw Charley Pride for the first time.

Ralph Fisher, a nationally known rodeo clown, performed at the rodeo when President LBJ came to Johnson City to hear Charley Pride sing and take in a rodeo back in 1968.

Charley Pride also tells this story every time he goes out on stage. He tells the story when he first performed on stage, the announcer introduced him; "Here comes Charley Pride!" The audience started clapping at first but when he came out, the crowd seeing that he was black, they would stop clapping. But when he lit into singing his favorite songs, the applause quickly came back. Charley Pride said he tells this story every time just before he starts his performance.

When Charley Pride first started out, they did not have any pictures of him with his songs. They were going to put him on "HEE HAW" television show, but they decided not to because he was black. So, they did not put any pictures out there of him when they first started selling his records. They did not put his pictures out there until he produced his first album.

Now, there was another story about how this white man saw Charley Pride cutting a yard in the all-white community of Highland Park in Dallas, Texas. The white man came up to Charley Pride and asked him how much he would charge to cut his yard. Charley gave him a price and went and cut the man's yard. A short time later, that same man saw Charley Pride performing on television singing his famous songs. He came back and told his friends that is the guy that mowed my yard—that was Charley Pride!

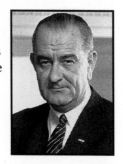

President Johnson was sitting up in the stands and he was sitting up about twelve feet from where I was working the bulls under the shoot. The President had a sky box right up on top and I said to myself, I see Charley Pride and President Lyndon Johnson right above me.

— CHAPTER 12 —

HOW GOD SHOWED UP ON
"THE GONG SHOW"

It took me six months to get on stage. To get on Cooter's Night Club version of THE GONG SHOW. Cooter's was a popular night club in the 1980's and had a version of THE GONG SHOW every Sunday night for the people. I watched the show for about two months. I went home and said I wanted to be on COOTER'S GONG SHOW. I went out and bought me a guitar.

I started practicing this one song. I said if I can get this one song, I can get the girls in the club. That is why I was doing this, to get the girls. I went home and started practicing every day. I got pretty good and started going to parks and beaches. I was really nervous. I would be playing my song as two or three people came by and listened to my song. If it were not no more than two or three people, I could do it.

I got good enough to take a chance to go to COOTER'S GONG SHOW. But as I was going to COOTER'S to appear on THE GONG SHOW, I was so nervous that if I were a tree, all the apples would shake off. As soon as THE GONG SHOW started, I just picked up my guitar and went out the front door.

After three months, I went back to Cooter's and told the guy I wanted to be on THE GONG SHOW. He asked me, "Were you here two or three months ago?" I said yes, but I had gotten so nervous and left. So, he entered me in COOTER'S GONG SHOW again; but as soon as they started the show, I got nervous and I left again.

So, about six months later, I came back to Cooter's again and said I wanted to be on THE GONG SHOW. This time, I stayed long enough for them to announce my name that I was going to be on THE GONG SHOW. When they said my name, I got nervous again and went out the back door.

About two months later, I was watching TV on a Christian station, and there was this black football player who was on it. I was listening to him when he shared his testimony that when he went from college football to the pros, he was so nervous that he would throw up about playing in the pros. So, he asked God to ease his nervousness so he could play. So, he prayed. At that time, he was living in an apartment without windows in it. Suddenly, a ray of sunlight hit his face. He looked down at his hands and they were not shaking as before. He was not nervous anymore. He shared that after that, he was able to play the best he had ever played. I said to myself, "That's what I want to happen to me."

So, the sun was shining through my window; It was shining in on me and I said, "God, please let this happen to me." The sun was feeling so good to me. But I was still nervous. So that night, I went up the stairs to put my contacts in and my hands were still shaking like a leaf on a tree. As I continued getting ready to go to Cooter's, I put my contacts in, but I was still shaking. So, I said, "God, God, please let me do this! I know I can do this." I got in my car and headed toward Cooter's. The closer I got to Cooter's, the more I would shake. So, I said, "God, let a car's headlight shine in my face and let me know I am ready." So, when I got to Cooter's, I went to the front and told the guys I wanted to be on THE GONG SHOW. He said, "Weren't you here a couple of times before and you left each time?" I told them, "Yeah, but this time I am not going to leave." I saw a girl that I had been dating and told her to not let me leave this time. "You hold on to me." She said, "Okay", and we went and sat down.

When they said THE GONG SHOW was starting, I started shaking again. THIS WAS BIG TIME SHAKING. I started leaving, but my girlfriend said you are not leaving this time. "You are going to face your fears." So, when they called my name, I do not know if you have ever been scared before, but I was so scared that my entire body was shaking even more. My guitar was trembling in my hands as I slowly walked up on the stage. The announcer said, "He is a little nervous folks, y 'all give him a little chance."

So, I sat in the chair. I had the guitar pick in my hands and immediately dropped it on the floor. It was so flat, and I was so nervous that I could not pick it up. I put my guitar on the floor, and I was so nervous that it made a vibrating sound. The announcer picked up my guitar pick and said again, "He's just a little nervous folks." So, I picked up my guitar and said, "God, please, please, let me know that I am ready." So, the announcer

then said, "This is Larry Callies doing Colorado Kool-Ade."
Then they shined a spotlight on me. I had never had a spotlight
to shine on me before. It warmed me up and then I heard a
voice say, "You ready!" I then looked at my hands and they
were not shaking anymore.

I looked out in the crowd. I started playing and it got quiet.
I was playing so well. I was imitating Johnny Paycheck to a,
"T"! What the people heard was a black man who sounded like
a white man. I began with, "We're sitting in this beer joint in
Houston, Texas, drinking Colorado Kool-Ade...." I had it down,
I had his voice down. The people were so intrigued. They were
saying, "Listen to him, He is good!" They were laughing at all
the jokes I was telling from the Colorado Kool-Ade song.

And then, suddenly, I started coming out of my body. I first
floated on the right side of my body. I could see my body
beneath me playing. I asked myself, "What's happening here?"
I could hear myself talking and I heard myself mess up. But
nobody else could tell that I had messed up. It was so quiet
in the building with over 2000 people in this club. And then, I
floated back in my body. It was very quiet and peaceful in the
club that night. The peace and quiet I witnessed that night was
something I had never seen before; and, I have not seen it since!

When I stopped playing, I heard the clapping of the people as
if they were in a theater instead of a nightclub because it was
so quiet and peaceful that night in the club. Something was
going on. I do not know what it was or why it happened even
to this day.

I just wanted to tell this story because I told this story on my documentary. This really happened. I won a trip to Mexico and a $1.000.00!

LARRY CALLIES—COUNTRY WESTERN SINGER. Two of Larry's favorite songs were "Amarillo by Morning" and "A Little Bit of Charlie in Me."

— CHAPTER 13 —

MY BRIEF CAREER AS A COUNTRY WESTERN SINGER

After high school graduation, I went to Wharton County Junior College. While I was there, I did participate in the Wharton County Junior College Rodeo. I got my feet wet in rodeo competition as I won some small little awards and jackpots at the black rodeos. But I was the Vice- President of the Wharton County Junior College Rodeo Club back in 1972.

I stayed at the college for about two years and then I quit and decided to get a job and go to work. I worked at the Baylor Co. which dealt with oil rigs and products. I worked there for a couple of years and then got a job working at the United States Post Office as a mailman. I spent 34 years working at the Post Office and retired in 2010.

I got back into the rodeo starting in 2000 and continued through 2010. From about 1980 to 2000, I entered a brief but promising singing career. I had entered a contest in 1984 and was in the top three winners out of 500 contestants at a Bear Creek Competition in Houston, Texas. That is when Roger Ramsey, with MCA Records, saw me at the contest. He then said he could get me in touch with George Strait's manager, Erv Woolsey. Two weeks before I was to sign the contract, I lost my voice to something called "vocal dysphonia"—it is a neurological disorder affecting the voice muscles in the larynx, or voice box or your vocal cords. I had to take Botox shots just to be able to talk for 24 years. Of course, this pretty much ended my singing career.

Before I lost my voice, I had my own group back in the early 1980's, and we sang with many well-known music artists of that day. The name of my group was called, LARRY CALLIES AND THE BRONCO BAND. This is the same band that COUNTRY WESTERN SINGER CLINT BLACK took over when LARRY CALLIES lost his voice.

Some of the bands we sang with were: IKIE SWEAT, who is famous for COTTON EYED JOE; we sang with ROY HEAD, a white singer who sang black music who was well known

LARRY CALLIES AND THE BRONCO BAND AT ITS BEGINNING.
The "Bronco Band" was formed in 1984. It has undergone changes in its composition over the years which included the fiddle players-- "Bob White," who played with Bob Wills and the Texas Playboys; and "Bob Rohan".

for the song which began, "I want to tell you a story...". Our group opened for famous people like CULLEN RAY; SELENA; TRAVIS TRITT; EMILIO, & JOHNNY RODRIGUEZ.

Larry Callies performed in many different venues with famous artists like Keith Junot, a country western artist. Larry opened for Roy Head, Pop & Soul artists at area concerts. (top right)

— CHAPTER 14 —

FROM COWBOY TO THE FOUNDER
OF THE BLACK COWBOY MUSEUM

After the tragedy with my voice, I got a job at the George Ranch, in Richmond, Texas, where I started working with saddle repair. I got so good at it; I eventually opened my own business working in saddle repair. Also, during this time, I got back into the rodeo circuit doing calf roping and team roping. Team roping is when two cowboys take down a steer with one focusing on roping the head and the other, roping the legs. I won many calf-roping and team roping championships from 1998 to 2017.

When I was young, during the 1970's, I also participated in bull riding. One year when I was at a rodeo in Fresno, Texas, as I was getting on the bull and I heard the voice of God say, "This is the last bull you will ride." I truly believed this was a message from God and that was the very last bull I rode.

While I was working at the George Ranch in Richmond, Texas, I was the lead cowboy at the ranch and again, I also worked on repairing saddles. One day, a young lady came by and took my picture while I was on my horse, Smooth. Her dad was with her and said his daughter took a picture of me and said she was going to paint it and enter it into the Houston Livestock Show and Rodeo Art Contest. I told him to tell her not to draw my picture because a picture of a black person had never won at the Houston Livestock Show and Rodeo in 35 years. And again, I thought that out of all the entries at the Houston Livestock Show and Rodeo, about 300,000, surely my picture would not win.

In 2011, Kimberly Agarwal, the young lady who painted my picture, won the Grand Prize in the art competition. Her painting of me sold for $205,000. They sold 3000 prints for $300.00 apiece. They made over a million dollars on my painting and I did not get a penny.

After I left the George Ranch, it was a short time later that I heard the voice of God again. It was about this same time, around 2016, that I was going through a personal problem in my life. I was now working in a saddle shop at City Farmer. It was around this time that I heard the voice of God again and He told me to step out on faith and open a Black Cowboy Museum.

Over the years beginning in 2011, while participating in rodeos and being in the cowboy environment, I had already started collecting artifacts related to the cowboy experience, particularly, the Black Cowboy experience. While I was working at City Farmer, I was able to work there for a couple more years before I started acting on the call to start a Black Cowboy Museum.

I opened the first Black Cowboy Museum at the intersection of Hwy 90 and Hwy 36, in a building right across the street from the EXXON gas station. We had a great, grand opening and it was then that I realized the great dream that God had given me was going to be even better than the first one I had.

Larry Callies welcomed family and friends from near and far at the grand opening of his museum on the corner of HWY 90 and HWY 36 in Rosenberg, Texas, June 2017. Over 250 people came out to this historic grand opening of THE BLACK COWBOY MUSEUM.

Some of the legendary black cowboys included Myrtis Dittman, Willie Thomas, Harold Cash, "Bailey Prairie Kid" , and Tex Williams.

Just before opening his museum, Larry Callies operated a Saddle Repair Shop in the back of City Farmer in Rosenberg, Texas, repairing saddles and doing leather work for family, friends, and strangers alike. He is well known for his quality saddle and leather work.

Sloan Williams, a well-known cattle rancher of Wharton, Texas, also attended the grand opening of The Black Cowboy Museum in 2017. Grady Allen, famed calf-roper from El Campo, Texas, (far right), donated a saddle to the museum.

Larry Callies worked for Sloan Williams as a young man and credited him for providing his first job opportunities to work with cattle and horses on a ranch and at rodeos.

— CHAPTER 15 —

LARRY CALLIES, HIS ROOTS WITH THE "OLD TEXAS 300" AND ENGLISH ROYALTY

When I first set out to open The Black Cowboy Museum, I went on TV on Channel 13 and said I wanted to open a black cowboy museum. This lady called me and told me she had a slave house she would like to donate to the museum. Her name was Naomi Mitchell Carrier. I noticed her middle name was Mitchell. I asked her where her middle name "Mitchell" came from because my mother's maiden name was also Mitchell. She said she was related to the Mitchell's from Hallettsville. I told her that my mother was also from Hallettsville. Then she said, "Well, Hello Cuz!" I asked her how does she know we were kin? She told me that we were descendants from a slave owner from Hallettsville, Texas, Captain Isaac Newton Mitchell. He was your great, great, great grandpa. I asked her, "how do you know this?" She said, there is an article on-line about Major James Kerr. In that article, you will find your great, great, great grandpa, Captain Isaac Newton Mitchell. He was the son-in-law of Captain James Kerr.

After she told me this, I had my son look up Captain James Kerr on the internet and he found a Texas family under the name of James Kerr. And when he did, I looked on page 11 and I saw my great, great, great grandpa, Captain Isaac Newton Mitchell. I did not have time to read it at home, so I took it to work the next day. While at work, my cousin, Dwight Callies from Edna, Texas, happened to walk in at the right time. He said, "What are you reading, Cuz?" I told him I was reading about my great, great, great grandpa, slave owner, Captain Isaac Newton Mitchell. Then he said, you need to read about the first slave owner in this article on page 2. And his name is James Kerr. He is your great, great, great grandpa, too! I said, what you talking about? He said, "Larry, all of the Callies come from Edna, Texas."

I remember what my dad had told me that all the Callies' came from Edna, Texas; and he warned me not to date any girls from Edna because, if I did, she would probably be my cousin. My cousin Dwight said you are probably right.

My cousin then told me that Major James Kerr was from Edna Texas, and he had several kids with slaves he owned. He was also a minister of the gospel. I asked my cousin, "How do you know he had kids with slaves?" He told me, "Just keep reading the article, Cuz." He remembered that on page 21 of the 22 pages in the article, it listed 12 kids that Major James Kerr had with slaves. He had documented everything about the births of his children in his bible. It was written that 6 of his 12 children were by Cynthia, his slave. I looked at all the slave names given in the article and then I called my Uncle Willie Callies from El Campo, Texas. Uncle Willie was born on June 19, 1919.

I said to my Uncle Willie, "How far can you go back in our family?" He said in a very, low voice, "We had a white grandma." My uncle was whispering on the telephone in 2013 like he feared someone overhearing what he was saying. I asked him again. Then he said again whispering, "We had a white grandma." I told Uncle Willie that I was going to come down from Beasley to come and see him. I drove to El Campo, Texas, with Naomi Mitchell Carrier to get first-hand knowledge about what Uncle Willie knew about our family. When we got there, we taped the conversation with Uncle Willie. He began sharing that his grandma was born, Annis on March 24, 1838. We continued the conversation and saved the information to document this history along with the article we had.

One day, I was talking with some people at the museum and I was sharing my family history with them. One of the ladies had come to the museum with her husband who did not want to come in and had remained in his car while his wife toured the museum, listening to my family history from Edna, Texas. She then asked me to stop so that she could get her husband out of the car. His name was Larry Patrick. Her name was Dianne. She left and went to her car and invited her husband who had been sitting in the car for about an hour to come in and listen to what I was sharing.

Larry Patrick came in and after listening to what I was saying about my family in Edna, Texas, he asked me if he could borrow the information I was sharing. I asked him why? He told me that he could trace my ancestors' history and he would bring back the information in about two weeks. I was a little hesitant to let him borrow the information I had, but I finally agreed to let him do this with the hopes that he would be able to trace my family's history and return my information.

In about a couple of weeks, Larry and his wife, Dianne, who had borrowed my family's history, came back with the history of all my ancestors. He began with my birth, my mother and father's birth and where we were born and continued to trace my family's history back to the 2nd, 4th, 8th, and as far back to the 14th generation. I was amazed when he revealed to me that I had royalty in my blood and was related to King Edward, IV and Queen Elizabeth of England.

When I share this with the visitors at the museum, I would say, "Since I come from kings and queens, you don't have to bow to me right now!" This would always get a laugh from the people listening. My new, found friend and historian then shared that Major James Kerr was one of the original "300" who came to Texas with Stephen F. Austin to settle Texas. So, I found out that I am also part of that history.

This guy had traced my ancestors all the way back to the early 1800's and found James Kerr's bible and it had everything in it. On one of the pages, there was a slave schedule from the 1850 census. On September 23, 1850, it listed Isaac Newton Mitchell had 28 slaves and he had 4 mulatto kids from those slaves. And one of them was my great, great, great, grandpa.

In the same article, it was listed that Major James Kerr had 17 slaves and from those slaves, he had 12 kids. Larry Patrick had traced my ancestors all the way back to 14 generations and gave me a binder with all this information in it from his research from Ancestry.com. I share this information from the binder with my guests at the Black Cowboy Museum.

During the first part of 2021, Bud Northington visited my museum. Bud Northington is a descendant of the Northington Plantation in Egypt, Texas, from the 1800's. He was looking through my ancestry book and he recognized that Major James Kerr, also a descendant of his, was in my book. He said, that since Major James Kerr was kin to me, then he was also kin to me. He started calling me, "Cuz".

Isaac Newton Mitchell II, direct descendant of Captain Isaac Newton Mitchell and ancestor of Larry Callies of THE BLACK COWBOY MUSEUM, is pictured on his ranch in Lolita, Texas during the mid-1800's.

Below are the "cowboys" at the end of a cattle drive penning the cattle at the Mitchell Ranch in Lolita, Texas and was also taken around the mid-1800's.

Two months ago, I get this phone call from San Marcos, Texas. The caller said that he was originally from Hallettsville. And he noticed that I had been looking on Ancestry.com looking up my family history. And he could tell that I was looking up information on the Mitchell family from Hallettsville. He told me that he was the great, great grandson of Captain Isaac Newton Mitchell. I got to talk with him for about 30 minutes. I noticed something strange in his voice. I asked if could ask him a personal question. And he said, yes. I said, "Are you white?" He said, "Yes, I am, Cuz!" And we continued the conversation, we said we would keep in contact with each other. And from that day on, we came the best of friends and cousins.

Larry Callies' "music DNA" like the "rodeo DNA", can be traced back through several generations of his family. Charley Willis, born in 1847, was a black cowboy who is credited with one of the famous old, country western tunes, "Goodbye Old Paint."

It is believed that Charley Willis would sing this song on the cattle drives in the mid-1800s which was later picked up by another cowboy, Jesse Morris, who played it on a fiddle throughout his life. He later recorded it in 1947 for the Library of Congress. "Goodbye Old Paint" is still sung by descendants of Charley Willis.

His name is Brian Mitchell. He sent me a picture over the phone, and I printed it out. I printed out his picture and placed it along with my 8 x 10 picture of myself, side by side. He shared with me that he wanted to move away from Hallettsville to east Texas. He loves to come down and visit with me. He told me that he has shared this information and discovery of his famous cousin, Larry Callies, with some of his people. I noticed that there are several things Brian and I have in common. Brian is a country singer and plays a guitar. I was a country singer with my own band until I lost my voice; but I still play the guitar. Brian was in a George Strait video. During the height of my career, George Strait manger was also my manager until I lost my voice. And Brian says he is a Christian and loves to sing Christian music. I have lived by my motto, "I am a Christian first and a Cowboy second."

Larry Callies (r), and Brian Mitchell (center), are distant cousins with relatives from Hallettsville, Texas. They both traced their ancestors to Captain Isaac Newton Mitchell, who owned slaves in the 1800's. Bud Northington (far right), was looking through Larry Callies ancestry book and discovered that Major James Kerr, a descendant of his, was also in Larry's book. Bud Northington then started calling Larry Callies, his cousin as well. Bud Northington is a descendant of the Northington Plantation in Egypt, Texas, from the 1800's. (Pictured with Larry are Bud Northington and his wife, Mary).

ADDITIONAL PICTURES
OF THE FIRST YEARS OF
THE BLACK COWBOY MUSEUM

ADDITIONAL PICTURES
OF THE FIRST YEARS OF
THE BLACK COWBOY MUSEUM

Here Comes Cowboy Larry, Stepping Out In Faith

AUTHORS
Larry Callies (r) and Michael D. Buford (l)

ABOUT THE AUTHORS

Larry Callies—Founder/CEO of The Black Cowboy Museum, was born on November 1952 in El Campo, Texas. He graduated from Boling High School and attended Wharton County Junior College before pursuing a Country Western Singing Career.

He was the founder of Larry Callies and The Bronco Band which he performed in many venues before he lost his voice. He was once being managed by George Strait's manager. Some of his many singing engagements were before government officials including President George W. Bush, Governor Ann Richards, local and state officials, and many of the Houston Mayors over the last 30 years.

He is also an accomplished rodeo calf and team roping Cowboy having won many trophies, championship belt buckles, and cash. Larry has been featured in the New York Times, Texas Monthly, and the Houston Chronicle. The Texas Country Reporter recorded a documentary on Larry, and he has been interviewed by other media regarding the history of the Black Cowboy which he has done extensive research before opening his famous, **THE BLACK COWBOY MUSEUM.**

Michael D. Buford, Founder/Publisher of The Good News Monthly, was born July 1952, in Charleston, South Carolina. He graduated from North Dallas High School and Texas A&M University. After serving as an educator, pastor, and publisher of a Christian newspaper, he retired and started working with Larry Callies and his museum in 2018. He is currently the Program/ Marketing Director of The Black Cowboy Museum.

BIBLIOGRAPHY

Callies, Leon. Interview. Interview conducted by Larry Callies. 1972.

Williams, "Preacher". Interview conducted by Larry Callies, 1974.

Callies, "Little Preacher". Interview conducted by Larry Callies, 1974.

Williams, "Tex". Interview conducted by Larry Callies, 1976.

Callis, Dwight. Interview conducted by Larry Callies, 2013.

Callies, Willie. Interview conducted by Larry Callies, 2013.

Mitchell Carrier, Naomi. Interview conducted by Larry Callies, 2013.

Adams, Marjorie. Interview conducted by Larry Callies, 2016.

Thomas, Willie, Interview conducted by Larry Callies, 2017.

Dittman, Myrtis, Interview conducted by Larry Callies, 2017.

Bailey, "Prairie Kidd". Interview conducted by Larry Callies, 2017. Patrick, Larry. Interview conducted by Larry Callies, 2019. (Ancestry.com)

Mitchell, Brian. Interview conducted by Larry Callies, 2019.

Northington, Bud. Interview conducted by Larry Callies, 2019.

Massey, Sarah R. (edited). BLACK COWBOYS OF TEXAS. Texas A&M University Press. 2004

O'Connor, Louise S. CRYIN' FOR DAYLIGHT, A Ranching Culture in The Texas Coastal Bend, 2nd edition. Wexford Publishing, 2007.

"Earliest American Cowboys Came from Houston." The George Ranch Historical Park.

PHOTO CREDITS

1. Larry Callies on his favorite horse, Mister Smooth (Cover Page: HLS&R)
2. Larry Callies on his favorite horse, Mister Smooth (P 4: HLS&R)
3. Larry Callies on a Southeast Texas ranch-(P 6: Harold Simmons Collection)
4. Larry Callies at the George Ranch, Richmond, TX (P 8: Harold Simmons)
5. Picture Collage: "I always wanted to be a cowboy." (P 10: Steve Magoon collection, Harold Simmons.)
6. Texas State Historical Association, Public domain, via Wikimedia Commons. (P 12: Black Cowboys)
7. Young Larry Callies and Old Grade School Building. (P 13: Callies & Buford)
8. Larry Callies and cousin, Tex Williams, steer roping on ranch. (P 14: Steve Magoon collection)
9. Larry Callies in calf-roping competition at rodeo. (P 15: Rodeo Arena photo)
10. Picture Collage: "My father said I was born with a veil over my eyes…" (P 16: picture of newborn baby with veil: www.quord.com; toddler picking cotton-Wikemedia Commons; Larry Callies in 3rd grade: Callies)
11. Larry with two brothers in Boling, TX. (P 20: Callies)
12. Black family picking cotton in the South. (P 21: Wikimedia Commons)
13. Picture Collage: East Bernard River, Known as the "Blue Hole," and a horse. (P 22: Buford and Steve Magoon)
14. Picture of a black panther. (P 25: dreamstime.com*)
15. Picture collage-"At the Rodeo"-(P 26: Cowboy getting ready to calf rope-Buford; Black cowboy bull riding-Callies; "Penning bulls"-Wikimedia Commons."
16. The "meanest bull around." (P 29: Black cowboy riding THE BEATLE-Sloan Williams collection)
17. Ralph Fisher and his trained buzzards. (P 32: Ralph Fisher, famous rodeo clown collection)
18. Bull Butting/Bull fighting (P 34: Tujavah-www.Trawell.in)
19. 2White Lightning. (P 37: The Black Cowboy Museum Collection)
20. V61 known as "Slim Jim" (P 39: The Black Cowboy Museum Collection)
21. Wild white cows. (P 40: readwriteandclick10.blogspot.com
22. Larry Callies, know as "Cowboy Larry," take a ride in country. (P 44: Steve Magoon collection)
23. "Looking back, I believe He has been watching over me…" (P 45: ***)
24. Wade in the Water. The tradition of Southern African Americans. (P 46: blackthen.com)
25. Wade in the Water images in Pinterest. (P 49: www.pinterest.com)
26. Damien Krushal, champion young bull rider from Wharton, TX. (P 50: Donald Krushal collection)
27. At the black cowboy rodeos, rhythm and blues singers, groups,…(REPLACEMENT PICTURE 1-BLACK RODEO - P 52: Buford)
28. Simonton, TX Rodeo champions in 1968. (P 53: Angleton Newspaper, 1968)
29. Larry attends Juneteenth Rodeo in Macbeth, TX at age of 15. (P 54: The Black Cowboy Museum Collection)
30. "I also got some praise from my mama when she said, "Boy, you did good!" (P 55 ***)
31. Larry Callies' first rodeo competition. (P 56: The Black Cowboy Museum collection)
32. Picture Coilage: Black cowboy being bucked off by a bull; Cowboy Larry practicing his calf roping skills. (P 59: Buford, Steve Magoon collection)
33. Larry Callies' Dad, Leon Callies, known as "Puggy". (P 60: The Black Cowboy Museum Collection)
34. "Puggy", Larry's Dad, calf-roping. (P 65: The Black Cowboy Museum Collection)
35. Mr. & Mrs. Leon Callies, Larry's parents, attending church at Mt. Scilla Baptist Church, Wharton, TX. (P 67: The Black Cowboy Museum collection)
36. Picture Collage-Cowboys in the family: Preacher Williams & Preacher Callies; Ike and Laval Callis, uncles. (P 68: The Black Cowboy Museum collection)
37. Picture Collage: Young TEX WILLIAMS riding a bull; Uncle Willie (cowboy) and Aunt Roberta of El Campo, TX; Dwight Callis, County Extension Agent for Texas A&M University and Mrs. Lorena Callis. (P 69: The Black Cowboy Museum collection)
38. Black cowboy in calf-roping competition at George Ranch. (P 70: Buford)
39. Picture Collage | Larry at rodeo during calf-roping event; Larry roping a steer on ranch. (P 71: TEAM ROPER'S RODEO and Steve Magoon collection)
40. Picture Collage-Larry's parents, Mr. Leon and Mrs. Inell Callies; and his baby sister, Valerie. (P 72: The Black Cowboy Museum Collection)
41. Picture Collage: Mrs. Inell Callies and three sons, Marvin, Leon, Jr., and Larry. (P 74: The Black Cowboy Museum collection)
42. Larry Callies, country western singer, comes back home to show his mother his brand-new Ford Bronco. (P 75: The Black Cowboy Museum collection)
43. Larry Callies begins his museum presentation with, "I am a Christian first and a Cowboy second!" (P 77: Buford)
44. Picture Collage | Charley Pride, Country music singer. (P 78: Wikipedia.org (P ublic domain). (REPLACEMENT PICTURE); LYRICS OF CHARLEY PRIDES FAVORITE SONG, "ANYBODY GOING TO SAN ANTOINE?" ON A TEXAS MAP SHOWING SAN ANTONIO, TX. (REPLACEMENT PICTURE)
45. Ralph Fisher and Don Schulze, famous rodeo clowns. (P 80: Ralph Fisher, RODEO CLOWN, collection)

46. President Lyndon B. Johnson. (P 81: Wikimedia Commons).

47. Picture Collage: Larry Callies-Country & Western singer early years; the Gong Show. (P 82: The Black Cowboy Museum collection; Wikipedia.org)

48. Larry Callies and the Bronco Band performs at GILLEY'S. (P 87: The Black Cowboy Museum collection)

49. Picture Collage | Larry Callies and the Bronco Band performing at Bear Creek Rodeo; Larry performing at the Soda Fountain in downtown Rosenberg, TX.
    (P 88: Harold Simmons collection; Steve Magoon collection)

50. The "original Larry Callies and the Bronco Band" started in 1984. (P 90: The Black Cowboy Museum collection).

51. Picture collage-Larry Callies, Country & Western singer; Larry with Roy Head, famous PoP and Soul Artist; Larry with Keith Junot, famous country western artist. (P 91: The Black Cowboy Museum collection and Steve Magoon Collection)

52. Larry Callies on a ranch in Southeast Texas getting ready to calf rope. (P 92: Steve Magoon collection).

53. Picture Collage | Grand Opening of The Black Cowboy Museum, Rosenberg, TX, June 2017; The Black Cowboy Museum new location two months later.
    (P 95: The Black Cowboy Museum collection)

54. Picture Collage | Larry Callies working in his new business before opening the museum, a saddle shoP was located in South Rosenberg, TX;
    Over 200 family and friends came to the grand opening in 2017. (P 96: The Black Cowboy Museum)

55. Picture collage-Sloan Williams and Grady Allen, Southeast Texas ranchers, at the grand opening of The Black Cowboy Museum; Larry's brother, Marvin, his cousin, Tex Williams, Congressman Phil Stephenson were among the guests at the 2017 grand opening. (P 97: Harold Simmons collection)

56. Picture collage-Major James Kerr, Captain Isaac Newton Mitchell and wife, former slave owners, are descendants of Larry Callies; Larry Callies demonstrates roping skills on his favorite horse, Mister Smooth. (P 98: The Black Cowboy Museum and Ancestry.com)

57. Picture collage-Isaac Newton Mitchell, II; and the Mitchell Ranch in Lolita, TX. (P 103: Brian Mitchell collection)

58. Charlie Willis (black cowboy), and wife. (P 104: courtesy of the BLACK PAST)

59. Larry Callies with cowboy cousin, Brian Mitchell, and cousin Bud Northington, descendant of the Northington Plantation of Egypt, TX.
    (P 105: Brian Mitchell, Buford)

60. Picture collage: Youth at The Black Cowboy Museum; Larry portraying Nat Love, Houston Livestock Show & Rodeo picture of Larry;
    Larry with Roy Head; guests at the museum. (P 106: Harold Simmons, Buford)

61. Picture collage: Larry wins trophy at rodeo; guest coming to the museum by bus, pre-pandemic large groups attending museum in 2018-19.
    (P 107: The Black Cowboy Museum, Buford)

62. Authors of the book, Larry Callies and Michael D. Buford. (P 108: The Black Cowboy Museum collection)

63. Young Larry Callies won many trophies and belt buckles for competing in rodeo events. (P 10: The Black Cowboy Museum Collection)

64. Larry Callies today, Founder/CEO of THE BLACK COWBOY MUSEUM. (P 112: Steve Magoon Collection)

65. Cowboy Larry with his advertising friend, "Cowboy Cody". (P 114: The Black Cowboy Museum Collection)

66. Cowboy Larry prepares to give another presentation in his museum. (P 116: Steve Magoon Collection)

How to Visit
The Black Cowboy Museum!

The Black Cowboy Museum, located at 1104 3rd Street, Rosenberg, Texas, is the only "Black Cowboy Museum" of its kind in the world.

THE BLACK COWBOY MUSEUM, (a 501 C 3 Non-profit organization) was founded by Larry Callies in July 2017. The museum is dedicated to the preservation of historical documents, memorabilia, artifacts, and pictures highlighting the rich history and amazing stories of the Black Cowboy of the Old West and exhibits the contributions, history, and cultures of all cowboys of the Old West, especially the amazing Cowboys of the great state of Texas.

"Cowboy Larry" is known by local residents and thousands of visitors from all across the globe, opened the museum using only his personal retirement money. Through the grace of God, THE BLACK COWBOY MUSEUM has fast become one of TRIP ADVISOR'S highly rated Southeast Texas tourist attractions and point of interest.

Contact The Black Cowboy Museum

Larry Callies, Founder/CEO

1104 3rd Street, Rosenberg, Texas 77471

281-787-3308

www.blackcowboymuseum.com

E-Mail:
clcallies@gmail.com

Follow Us On Instagram:
theblackcowboymuseum

Follow Us On Facebook
theblackcowboymuseum

One of Southeast Texas great tourist attractions!

From the praise and accolades from tourists, church groups, public and private schools, and city and county governments, THE BLACK COWBOY MUSEUM is a great museun to visit - offering interesting, exciting, and educational information for all ages!

Hours
Tues – Sat
9:00 AM – 5:00 PM
(Special Tours by Appointment)

Admission
Adults: $10
Seniors: 65 & Up: $7.00
Children: 6 – 12: $7.00
Children 5 & Under: Free